THE TONGUES OF MEN & OF ANGELS

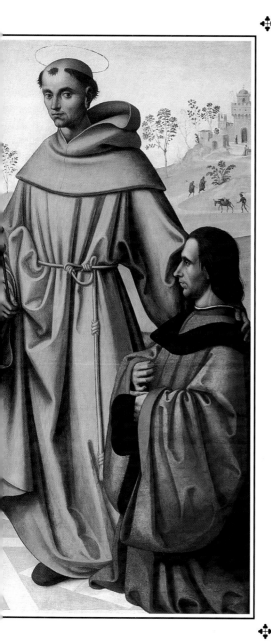

The Tongues of Men & of Angels

Inspirational Poetry & Prose from the Renaissance to the Restoration

EDITED BY
JAMES BENTLEY

THE INCREDULITY OF ST THOMAS,
Giovanni Battista da Faenza

A Bulfinch Press Book
LITTLE, BROWN AND COMPANY
Boston · New York · Toronto · London

Text and compilation copyright © 1996 by James Bentley

First Edition

ISBN 0-8212-2336-4

Extracts from the Authorized Version of the Bible
(The King James Bible), the rights in which are vested
in the Crown, are reproduced by permission of the
Crown's Patentee, Cambridge University Press.
Please see page 120 for further acknowledgements

A CIP catalogue record for this book
is available from the British Library
Library of Congress Catalog Number 96-84339

Decorative illustrations by Nadine Wickenden
Designed by David Fordham

Published simultaneously in the United States of America by Bulfinch Press,
an imprint and trademark of Little, Brown and Company (Inc.),
in Great Britain by Little, Brown and Company (UK),
and in Canada by Little, Brown & Company (Canada) Limited

PRINTED IN SINGAPORE

CONTENTS

INTRODUCTION

✠

The title of this anthology derives from one of the acknowledged masterpieces of English prose: the Authorized (or the King James) Version of the Bible, which was published in 1611 and superbly translates St Paul's magnificent eulogy of Charity. The passage begins, 'Though I speak with the tongues of men and of angels, and have not charity, I am become as sounding brass or a tinkling cymbal,' and ends, 'And now abideth faith, hope and charity, these three; but the greatest of these is charity.'

The National Gallery, whose sixteenth- and seventeenth-century collection is rich enough to supply illustrations for the whole of this volume, has a superb painting of *Charity* by Anthony van Dyck, worthy to stand by Thomas Cranmer's supplication, from the 1549 Book of Common Prayer, which declares that 'all our doings without charity are nothing worth.'

This is the quality of religious prose and poetry and great works of art to be harvested from the sixteenth and seventeenth centuries. Remarkably, the King James Version of the Bible was the work not of one person but of a committee. One of the authors included in this anthology, John Selden, described it as 'the best Translation in the World'. The translators, he added, took an excellent way. 'That part of the Bible was given to him who was most excellent in such a tongue (as the *Apocrypha* to *Andrew Downs*) and then they met together, and one read the Translation, the rest holding in their hands some Bible, either of the learned Tongues, or *French, Spanish, Italian, &c.* If they found any Fault, they spoke; if not, he read on.'

Yet they based their work on a previous translation made by one man, the martyr William Tyndale, a work which in some ways surpasses in excellence and oratory all subsequent translations. As the revisers of the New Testament in 1880 generously and rightly put it, 'The foundation was laid by William Tyndale. His translation of the New Testament

was the true primary Version. The Versions that followed were either substantially reproductions of Tyndale's translation in its final shape, or revisions of Versions that had been themselves almost entirely based on it.' Whenever I have used a passage of Holy Scripture where in my view Tyndale's Version is finer than that of 1611, I have turned to Tyndale, and modernized only the spellings.

The first section of this anthology encompasses some of the greatest Biblical stories and themes, drawn from the Old Testament and the New, in part taken from these two translations. All of them are splendidly illustrated in the National Gallery's collection, often by the greatest contemporary artists. Rembrandt, for example, painted *Belshazzar's Feast*. Titian produced an entrancing *Noli me Tangere*, which, placed here with Tyndale, would also match the writings of Jeremy Taylor, who described the Virgin Mary standing 'sad, silent, and with a modest grief, deep as the waters of the abysse, but smooth as the face of a Pool, full of love, and patience, and sorrow, and hope.'

William Tyndale believed that reading and meditating on the New Testament would either bring one to salvation or else to damnation. As he insisted, 'For the nature of God's word is, that whosoever reade it or hear it reasoned and disputed before him, it will begin immediately to make him every day better and better, till he be grown into a perfect man in the knowledge of Christ and love of the law of God: or else make him worse and worse, till he be hardened that he openly resist the spirit of God, and then blaspheme, after the ensample of Pharao, Coza, Abiron, Balam, Judas, Symon Magus and such other.'

This was a view shared by most of his contemporaries, and the second and third sections of this anthology are therefore devoted to virtues and vices. Among virtues, alongside charity human faithfulness, for example, is represented by Spenser's poem *Amoretti*:

> So let us love, dear love, like as we ought,
> love is the lesson which the Lord us taught.

a poem complemented by the fourth of Paolo Veronese's *Allegories of Love*: a couple beside a cornucopia and accompanied by a dog (the symbol of fidelity). As for the virtue of mercy, Shakespeare's 'The quality of mercy is not strained', is matched by Luca Signorelli's *Coriolanus persuaded by his Family to spare Rome*.

Patience, another virtue in this book, is movingly espoused in John Milton's poem on his own blindness, which I have contrasted with Palma Vecchio's *Portrait of a Poet*, whose eyes are not only dreamy but also sharp and observant.

Believing that their fate in the next world depended on their virtue or viciousness in this, men and women in the sixteenth and seventeenth century developed powerful moral opinions. So Francis Bacon's essay 'Of Riches' eloquently condemned greed, declaring:

> I cannot call *Riches* better, than the Baggage of Vertue.
> The *Roman* Word is better, *Impedimenta*. For as the Baggage
> is to an Army, so is Riches to Vertue. It cannot be spared,
> nor left behinde, but it hindreth the March.

Similarly, voluptuousness, vain delights, covetousness and the like were excoriated by these writers. As, for example, Marinus van Reymerswaele's grotesque caricature of *Two Taxgatherers* reveals, the artists of the era could be equally savage in depicting vice.

My final section is called 'This World and the Next'. It speaks, of course, of the resurrection of the dead. John Donne's *Divine Poems* include the most triumphalist attack on death, beginning:

> Death be not proud, though some have called thee
> Mighty and dreadfull, for, thou art not soe.

and ending: death, thou shalt die.

Its accompanying image is *A Young Man holding a Skull* by Frans Hals.

Less triumphalist but of the equally powerful pieces in this section will be George Herbert's poem, 'Love':

> Love bade me welcome; yet my soul drew back,
> Guilty of dust and sin,

which ends: 'You must sit down,' says Love, 'and taste my Meat.'
> So I did sit and eat.

a poem that joins heaven to earth at the Holy Communion. And this is illustrated by Caravaggio's *Supper at Emmaus*.

John Donne's writings illuminate part of the contemporary explosion of ideas and knowledge which helped to create the minds of whose who produced these remarkable verses and paragraphs.

Navigators had proved that the earth was round; but traditionally the earth was supposed to have four corners where the angels would blow their trumpets announcing the end of the world and the final resurrection. Donne knew the earth was round, but in one of his sonnets wished to call on the angels to announce, from these non-existent corners, this last day. He audaciously solved the problem with one word: 'imagined':

> At the round earths imagin'd corners, blow
> Your trumpets, Angells . . .

Over the two centuries covered by this anthology the hearts of these writers and artists were also tugged to and fro by the conflicts of the Reformation, the Civil War, the execution of a king and the restoration of another. Some of these authors suffered imprisonment and exile – and in the case of Tyndale, Archbishop Thomas Cranmer and Sir Walter Ralegh, execution. Faith was not for them a trivial matter.

Like Donne, they developed unrivalled techniques for heightening the impact of what they wrote. One gift was for simile and metaphor, such as the Puritan preacher Samuel Ward utilized in a sermon of 1622 which describes drunkards as 'walking like the tops of trees shaken with the winds, like masts of Ships reeling on the tempestuous Seas.' Many possessed an aptitude for biting satire, such as Jeremy Taylor deployed when he observed that, 'He that is proud of riches is a fool; For if he be exalted above his neighbours, because he hath more gold, how much inferior is he to a gold mine!'

Another especially powerful rhetorical technique, that of cumulative repetition, is witnessed to by Tyndale's translation of St John's description of Mary Magdalen, weeping beside the sepulchre of Jesus because she cannot find his body. I have set alongside this extremely moving passage Titian's *Noli Me Tangere*, in which the Magdalen lies faltering before her lord.

Other artists represented here reached the same heights of religious genius as Titian, particularly Michelangelo, Rubens and Rembrandt. As well as these masters, this anthology is able to draw on the works of Bellini and Caravaggio, and of such scarcely lesser masters as Giovanni Palma, Jan Gossaert, Hans Holbein the Younger and Annibale Carracci.

The authors included in this book range from Edmund Spenser to John Dryden and of course include Shakespeare, Robert Herrick and George Herbert as well as John Milton and John Bunyan, who (like Donne) wrote both poetry and prose. No such anthology could omit such masters of religious prose as Francis Bacon, Sir Thomas Browne, whose *Religio Medici* (the Religion of a Physician) appeared in 1635, and Jeremy Taylor, author of *Rule and Excercises of Holy Living* and *Holy Dying*.

These writers and artists were also learned, but by no means recluses. John Milton will serve as an example for many of them. He read Hebrew, Greek, Latin, Italian, French and Spanish, and when he went blind his daughter would read to him works by Ovid and Euripides in the original tongue.

Though blind, his daily routine, like that of many others represented here, was rich. As Dr Samuel Johnson noted, 'When he first rose he heard a chapter in the Hebrew Bible, and then studied till twelve; then took some exercise for an hour; then dined; then played on the organ and sung, or heard another sing; then studied to six; then entertained his visitors till eight; then supped; and, after a pipe of tobacco and a glass of water, went to bed.' Dr Johnson also wrote rumbustiously of Milton's married life. 'All his wives were virgins; for he has declared that he thought it gross and indelicate to be a second husband: upon what other principles his choice was made, cannot now be known; but marriage afforded him not much of his happiness. The first wife left him in disgust, and was brought back only by terror; the second, indeed, seems to have been more a favourite, but her life was short. The third . . . oppressed his children in his lifetime, and cheated them at his death.'

Yet in *Paradise Lost* Milton evoked a portrait of Eve which, he wrote, inspired, 'The spirit of love and amorous delight'. Eve, he gloriously asserted, was moulded by God:

> Under his forming hands a Creature grew,
> Manlike, but different sex, so lovely faire,
> That what seemd fair in all the World seemd now
> Mean, or in her summed up, in her contained
> And in her looks, which from that time infused
> Sweetness into my heart, unfelt before,
> And into all things from her Aire inspired
> The spirit of love and amorous delight.

Rich and sometimes harrowing experiences inform these works. Could Patrick Carey have written about Jesus's agony before his crucifixion and Garofalo illustrated it, had they not experienced suffering? Could George Herbert have written, 'Love bade me welcome,' had he himself not been welcomed by love?

JAMES BENTLEY 1996

THE HERITAGE OF THE BIBLE

IN HEAVEN BE GLORY,
PEACE UNTO THE EARTH!

WILLIAM DRUMMOND OF HAWTHORNDEN

ADORATION OF THE SHEPHERDS, *Bernardino da Asola*

BELSHAZZAR'S FEAST, *Rembrandt*

BELSHAZZAR'S FEAST

✠

BELSHAZZAR THE KING made a great feast to a thousand of his Lords, and drank wine before the thousand . . . Then they brought the golden vessels that were taken out of the temple of the house of God which was at Jerusalem; and the king, and his princes, his wives, and his concubines, drank in them. They drank wine, and praised the gods of gold, and of silver, of brass, of iron, of wood, and of stone.

In the same hour came forth fingers of a man's hand, and wrote over against the candlestick upon the plaster of the wall of the king's palace: and the king saw the part of the hand that wrote.

Then the king's countenance was changed, and his thoughts troubled him, so that the joints of his loins were loosed, and his knees smote one against the other . . .

Then was Daniel brought in before the king . . . and said before the king . . . [Thou] hast lifted up thyself against the Lord of heaven; and they have brought the vessels of his house before thee, and thou, and thy lords, thy wives, and thy concubines, have drunk wine in them; and thou hast praised the gods of silver, and gold, of brass, iron, wood, and stone, which see not, nor hear, nor know: and the God in whose hand thy breath is, and whose are all thy ways, thou hast not glorified . . .

And this is the writing that was written, MENE, MENE, TEKEL, UPHARSIN. This is the interpretation of the thing: MENE; God hath numbered thy kingdom, and finished it. TEKEL; Thou art weighed in the balances, and found wanting. PERES; Thy kingdom is divided, and given to the Medes and Persians.

Then commanded Belshazzar, and they clothed Daniel with scarlet, and put a chain of gold about his neck, and made a proclamation concerning him, that he should be the third ruler in the kingdom.

In that night was Belshazzar the king of the Chaldeans slain.

DANIEL V, THE KING JAMES VERSION OF THE BIBLE

CHRIST IN THE GARDEN

Look, how he glows for heat!
What flames come from his eyes!
'Tis blood that he does sweat,
Blood his bright forehead dyes:
See, see! It trickles down:
Look, how it showers amain!
Through every pore
His blood runs o'er,
And empty leaves each vein.
His very heart
Burns in each part;
A fire his breast doth sear:
For all this flame,
To cool the same
He only breathes a sigh, and weeps a tear.

Patrick Carey

THE AGONY IN THE GARDEN, *Garofalo*

THE PURIFICATION OF THE TEMPLE, *Jacopo Bassano*

The
Cleansing of the Temple

They come to Jerusalem: and Jesus went into the temple, and began to cast out them that sold and bought in the temple, and overthrew the tables of the moneychangers, and the seats of them that sold doves;

And would not suffer that any man should carry any vessel through the temple.

And he taught, saying unto them, Is it not written, My house shall be called of all nations the house of prayer? but ye have made it a den of thieves.

And the Scribes and chief priests heard it, and sought how they might destroy him: for they feared him, because all the people was astonished at his doctrine.

MARK XI,
THE KING JAMES VERSION OF THE BIBLE

Noli me Tangere

✠

Mary stood without at the sepulchre weeping. And as she wept, she bowed herself into the sepulchre and saw two angels in white sitting, the one at the head and the other at the feet, where they had laid the body of Jesus. And they said unto her: woman, why weepest thou? She said unto them: For they have taken away my lord, and I wot not where they have laid him. When she had thus said, she turned herself back and saw Jesus standing, and knew not that it was Jesus. Jesus said unto her: woman, why weepest thou? Whom seekest thou? She supposing that he had been the gardener, said unto him: Sir if thou have borne him hence tell me where thou hast laid him, that I may fetch him. Jesus said unto her: Mary. She turned herself and said unto him: Rabboni, which is to say master. Jesus said unto her, touch me not, for I am not yet ascended to my father. But go to my brethren and say unto them, I ascend unto my father and your father too: my god and your god. Mary Magdalene came and told the disciples that she had seen the lord, and that he had spoken such things unto her.

JOHN XX,
TRANSLATED BY
WILLIAM TYNDALE

CHRIST APPEARING TO THE MAGDALEN (*NOLI ME TANGERE*), *Titian*

A LANDSCAPE WITH A SHEPHERD AND HIS FLOCK, *Peter Paul Rubens*

THE LORD IS MY SHEPHERD

THE LORD IS MY SHEPHERD; therefore can I lack nothing.

He shall feed me in a green pasture: and lead me forth beside the waters of comfort.

He shall convert my soul: and bring me forth in the paths of righteousness, for his Name's sake.

Yea, though I walk through the valley of the shadow of death, I will fear no evil: for thou art with me; thy rod and thy staff comfort me.

Thou shalt prepare a table before me against them that trouble me: thou hast anointed my head with oil; and my cup shall be full.

But thy loving-kindness and mercy shall follow me all the days of my life: and I will dwell in the house of the Lord for ever.

PSALM XXIII, THE 1549 BOOK OF COMMON PRAYER,
THOMAS CRANMER

The Angels
for the
Nativity of Our Lord

Run, shepherds, run where Bethlem blest appears,
We bring the best of news, be not dismayed,
A Saviour there is born more old than years,
Amidst heaven's rolling heights this earth who stayed.
In a poor cottage inned, a virgin maid
A weakling did him bear, who all upbears;
There is he, poorly swaddled, in manger laid,
To whom too narrow swaddlings are our spheres:
Run, shepherds run, and solemnize his birth,
This is that night – no, day, grown great with bliss,
In which the power of Satan broken is;
In heaven be glory, peace unto the earth!
    Thus singing, through the air the angels swam,
    And cope of stars re-echoèd the same.

WILLIAM DRUMMOND OF HAWTHORNDEN

THE HOLY FAMILY AND A SHEPHERD, *Titian*

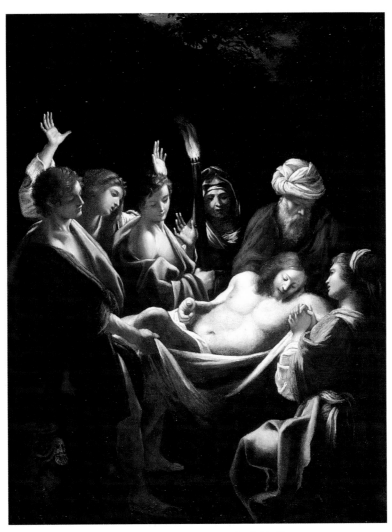

CHRIST CARRIED TO THE TOMB, *Sisto Badalocchio*

THE ENTOMBMENT OF JESUS

✠

JESUS CRIED WITH A LOUD VOICE, and gave up the ghost. And the veil of the temple did rend in two pieces, from the top to the bottom. And when the Centurion which stood before him, saw that he so cried and gave up the ghost, he said: truly this man was the son of God. There were also women a good way off beholding him: among whom was Mary Magdalen, and Mary the mother of James the little and of Ioses, and Mary Salome which also when he was in Galilee, followed him and ministered unto him, and many other women which came up with him to Jerusalem.

And now when night was come (because it was the even that goeth before the Sabbath) Joseph of Arimathea, a noble counsellor, which also looked for the kingdom of God, came and went in boldly unto Pilate; and begged the body of Jesu. And Pilate marvelled that he was already dead, and called unto him the Centurion, and asked of him, whether he had been any while dead. And when he knew the truth of the Centurion, he gave the body to Joseph. And he brought a linen cloth, and took him down and wrapped him in the linen cloth, and laid him in a tomb that was hewn out of the rock, and rolled a stone unto the door of the sepulchre. And Mary Magdalen and Mary Ioses beheld where he was laid.

MARK XV,
TRANSLATED BY
WILLIAM TYNDALE

THE TREE OF KNOWLEDGE

THE SACRED TREE midst the fair orchard grew;
    The phoenix truth did on it rest
    And built his perfumed nest.
That right Porphyrian tree which did true logic show
    Each leaf did learnèd notions give,
    And the apples were demonstrative:
    So clear their colour and divine
The very shade they cast did other lights outshine.

Taste not, said God, 'Tis mine and angels' meat:
    A certain death doth sit
    Like an ill worm i' the core of it.
Ye cannot know and live, nor live or know and eat.
    Thus spoke God, yet man did go
    Ignorantly on to know;
    Grew so more blind, and she
Who tempted him in this grew yet more blind than he.

The only science man by this did get
    Was but to know he nothing knew:
    He straight his nakedness did view,
His ignorant, poor estate, and was ashamed of it.
    Yet searches probabilities
    And rhetoric and fallacies,
    And seeks by useless pride
With slight and withering leaves that nakedness to hide.

Henceforth, said God, the wretched sons of earth
    Shall sweat for food in vain
    That will not long sustain
And bring with labour forth each fond abortive birth.
    That serpent too, their pride,
    Which aims at things denied;
    That learned and eloquent lust
Instead of mounting high shall creep upon the dust.

ABRAHAM COWLEY

THE VIRGIN AND CHILD WITH SAINT ANNE, *Gerolamo dai Libri*

LANDSCAPE IN THE ROMAN CAMPAGNA WITH A MAN SCOOPING WATER, *Nicolas Poussin*

The World Was All Before Them

✠

THE BRANDISHED SWORD of God before them blazed
Fierce as a comet; which with torrid heat,
And vapour as the Libyan air adust,
Began to parch that temperate clime: whereat
In either hand the hastening angel caught
Our lingering parents; and to th'Eastern gate
Led them direct, and down the cliff as fast
To the subjected plain; then disappeared.
They looking back, all th'eastern side beheld
Of Paradise, so late their happy seat,
Waved over by that flaming brand, the gate
With dreadful faces thronged and fiery arms.
Some natural tears they dropped, but wiped them soon;
The world was all before them, where to choose
Their place of rest, and providence their guide:
They hand in hand with wandering steps and slow
Through Eden took their solitary way.

JOHN MILTON,
PARADISE LOST, BOOK XII

To His Saviour, a Child; a Present, by a Child

Go pretty child, and bear this flower
Unto thy little Saviour;
And tell him, by that bud now blown,
He is the *Rose of Sharon* known:
When thou hast said so, stick it there
Upon his bib, or stomacher:
And tell him, (for good handsel too)
That thou hast brought a whistle new,
To charm his cries, (at time of need:)
Tell him, for coral, thou hast none;
But if thou hadst, he should have one;
But poor thou art, and known to be
Even as moneyless, as he.
Lastly, if thou canst win a kiss
From those mellifluous lips of his.
Then never take a second one,
To spoil the first impression.

ROBERT HERRICK

THE VIRGIN AND CHILD WITH FLOWERS, *Carlo Dolci*

AN OLD MAN IN AN ARMCHAIR, *Rembrandt*

Vanity of Vanities

✠

Vanity of vanities, saith the Preacher, vanity of vanities, all is vanity.

What profit hath a man of all his labour which he taketh under the sun?

One generation passeth away, and another generation cometh: but the earth abideth for ever.

The sun also ariseth, and the sun goeth down, and hasteth to the place where he arose.

The wind goeth toward the south, and turneth about unto the north; it whirleth around continually, and the wind returneth again according to his circuits.

All the rivers run into the sea, yet the sea is not full; unto the place from whence the rivers came, thither they return again.

All things are full of labour; man cannot utter it: the eye is not satisfied with seeing, nor the ear filled with hearing.

The thing that hath been, it is that which shall be: and that which is done is that which shall be done: and there is no new thing under the sun . . .

I the Preacher was king over Israel in Jerusalem.

And I gave my heart to seek and search out by wisdom concerning all things that are done under heaven . . .

I communed with mine own heart, saying, Lo, I am come to great estate, and have gotten more wisdom than all they that have been before me in Jerusalem: yea, my heart had great experience of wisdom and knowledge.

And I gave my heart to know wisdom, and to know madness and folly: I perceived that this also is vexation of spirit.

For in much wisdom is much grief: and he that increaseth knowledge, increaseth sorrow.

Ecclesiastes I,
The King James Version of the Bible

VIRTUES

LOVE IS THE LESSON
WHICH THE LORD US TAUGHT

EDMUND SPENSER

MADONNA AND CHILD WITH SAINTS JOHN THE BAPTIST AND CATHERINE OF ALEXANDRIA, *Titian*

CHARITY

O LORD, who has taught us that all our doings without
charity are nothing worth; Send thy Holy Ghost, and pour
into our hearts that most excellent gift of charity,
the very bond of peace and all virtues, without which
whosoever liveth is counted dead before thee: Grant
this for thine only Son Jesus Christ's sake. *Amen.*

THE 1549 BOOK OF COMMON PRAYER,
THOMAS CRANMER

CHARITY, *Anthony van Dyck*

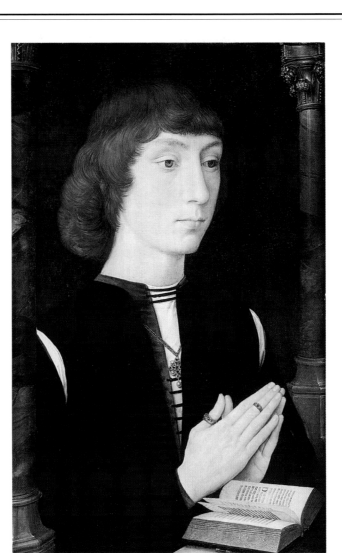

A YOUNG MAN AT PRAYER, *Hans Memlinc*

CONTENTMENT

How happy is he born and taught
That serveth not another's will;
Whose armour is his honest thought,
And simple truth his utmost skill!

   Whose passions not his masters are;
Whose soul is still prepared for death,
Untied unto the world by care
Of public fame or private breath;

   Who envies none that chance doth raise,
Nor vice; who never understood
How deepest wounds are given by praise;
Nor rules of state, but rules of good;

   Who hath his life from rumours freed;
Whose conscience is his strong retreat;
Whose state can neither flatterers feed,
Nor ruin make oppressors great;

   Who God doth late and early pray,
More of His grace than gifts to lend;
And entertains the harmless day
With a religious book or friend;

   — This man is freed from servile bands
Of hope to rise or fear to fall;
Lord of himself, though not of lands,
And having nothing, yet hath all.

HENRY WOTTON,
'THE CHARACTER OF A HAPPY LIFE'

LOVE

✠

Most glorious lord of life, that on this day,
   didst make thy triumph over death and sin:
   and, having harrowed hell, didst bring away
   captivity thence captive, us to win:
This joyous day, dear Lord, with joy begin,
   and grant that we for whom thou diddest die
   being with thy dear blood clean washed from sin,
   may live for ever in felicity.
And that thy love we weighing worthily,
   may likewise love thee for the same again:
   and for thy sake that all like dear didst buy,
   with love may one another entertain.
So let us love, dear love, like as we ought,
   love is the lesson which the Lord us taught.

EDMUND SPENSER, *Amoretti*

ALLEGORY OF LOVE, IV ('HAPPY UNION'), *Paolo Veronese*

PORTRAIT OF GOVAERT VAN SURPELE (?) AND HIS WIFE, *Jacob Jordaens*

The Glory of Marriage

Dearly beloved, we are gathered together here in the sight of God, and in the face of this congregation, to join together this Man and this Woman in holy Matrimony; which is an honourable estate, instituted of God in the time of man's innocency, signifying unto us the mystical union that is betwixt Christ and his Church: which holy estate Christ adorned and beautified with his presence, and first miracle that he wrought, in Cana of Galilee; and is commended of Saint Paul to be honourable among all men; and therefore is not by any to be enterprised, nor taken in hand, unadvisedly, lightly, or wantonly, to satisfy men's carnal lusts and appetites, like brute beasts that have no understanding: but reverently, discreetly, advisedly, soberly, and in the fear of God; duly considering the causes for which Matrimony was ordained.

First, it was ordained for the procreation of children, to be brought up in the fear and nurture of the Lord, and to the praise of his holy Name.

Secondly, it was ordained for a remedy against sin, and to avoid fornication: that such persons as have not the gift of continency might marry, and keep themselves undefiled members of Christ's body.

Thirdly, it was ordained for the mutual society, help, and comfort, that the one ought to have of the other, both in prosperity and adversity. Into which holy estate these two persons present come now to be joined. Therefore if any man can shew any just cause why they may not lawfully be joined together, let him now speak, or else hereafter for ever hold his peace.

The 1549 Book of Common Prayer,
Thomas Cranmer

THE GLORY OF WOMEN

✠

This Sex, in the Old Testament, coveted Children, if happily this or that Woman might be the Mother of the Saviour of the World. I will say again, that when the Saviour was come, Women rejoyced in him, before either Man or Angel. I read not that ever any man did give unto Christ so much as one Groat, but the Women followed him, and ministred to him of their Substance. 'Twas a Woman that washed his Feet with Tears, and a Woman that anointed his Body to the Burial. They were Women that wept when he was going to the Cross; and Women that followed him from the Cross, and that sat by his Sepulchre when he was buried. They were Women that was first with him at his Resurrection-morn, and Women that brought Tiding first to his Disciples that he was risen from the Dead. Women therefore are highly favoured, and shew by these things that they are sharers with us in the Grace of Life.

JOHN BUNYAN, *PILGRIMS PROGRESS*

THE DEAD CHRIST MOURNED ('THE THREE MARIES'), *Annibale Carracci*

CORIOLANUS PERSUADED BY HIS FAMILY TO SPARE ROME, *Luca Signorelli*

MERCY

The quality of mercy is not strain'd,
It droppeth as the gentle rain from heaven
Upon the place beneath: it is twice bless'd;
It blesseth him that gives and him that takes:
'Tis mightiest in the mightiest: it becomes
The throned monarch better than his crown;
His sceptre shows the force of temporal power,
The attribute to awe and majesty,
Wherein doth sit the dread and fear of kings;
But mercy is above this sceptred sway,
It is enthroned in the hearts of kings,
It is an attribute of God himself,
And earthly power doth then show likest God's
When mercy seasons justice.

WILLIAM SHAKESPEARE,
THE MERCHANT OF VENICE

OF TRUTH

✠

W HAT IS *TRUTH*; said jesting *Pilate*; And would not stay for an Answer. Certainly there be, that delight in Giddinesse; And count it a Bondage, to fix a Beleefe; Affecting Freewill in Thinking, as well as in Acting. And though the Sects of Philosophers of that Kinde be gone, yet there remaine certaine discoursing Wits, which are of the same veines, though there be not so much Bloud in them, as was in those of the Ancients. But it is not onely the Difficultie, and Labour, which Men take in finding out of *Truth*; Nor againe, that when it is found, it imposeth upon men's Thoughts; that doth bring *Lies* in favour: But a naturall, though corrupt Love, of the *Lie* it selfe. One of the later Schoole of the Grecians, examineth the matter, and is at a stand, to thinke what should be in it, that men should love *Lies*; Where neither they make for Pleasure, as with Poets; Nor for Advantage, as with the Merchant; but for the *Lies* sake. But I cannot tell: This same *Truth*, is a Naked, and Open day light, that doth not shew the Masques, and Mummeries, and Triumphs of the world, halfe so Stately, and daintily, as Candlelights. *Truth* may perhaps come to the price of a Pearle, that sheweth best by day: But it will not rise, to the price of a Diamond, or Carbuncle, that sheweth best in varied lights. A mixture of a *Lie* doth ever adde Pleasure.

FRANCIS BACON, *ESSAYES*

CHRIST BEFORE PILATE, *Master of Cappenberg*

THE GOOD SAMARITAN, *Jacopo Bassano*

THE GOOD SAMARITAN

✠

Jesus said, A certain man went down from Jerusalem to Jericho, and fell among thieves, which stripped him of his raiment, and wounded him, and departed, leaving him half dead.

And by chance there came down a certain priest that way: and when he saw him, he passed by on the other side.

And likewise a Levite, when he was at the place, came and looked on him, and passed by on the other side.

But a certain Samaritan, as he journeyed, came where he was: and when he saw him, he had compassion on him.

And went to him, and bound up his wounds, pouring in oil and wine, and set him on his own beast, and brought him to an inn, and took care of him.

And on the morrow when he departed, he took out two pence, and gave them to the host, and said unto him, Take care of him; and whatsoever thou spendest more, when I come again, I will repay thee.

Which now of these three, thinkest thou, was neighbour unto him that fell among the thieves?

And he said, He that shewed mercy on him. Then said Jesus to him, Go, and do thou likewise.

☆

Luke X,
The King James Version
of the Bible

ON HIS BLINDNESS

W<small>HEN</small> I <small>CONSIDER</small> how my light is spent,
   Ere half my days in this dark world and wide,
   And that one Talent which is death to hide,
   Lodged with me useless, though my Soul more bent
To serve therewith my Maker, and present
   My true account, lest he returning chide;
   Doth God exact day-labour, light denied?
   I fondly ask; but Patience to prevent
That murmur, soon replies, God doth not need
   Either man's work or his own gifts; who best
   Bear his mild yoke, they serve him best. His state
Is kingly. Thousands at his bidding speed
   And post o'er Land and Ocean without rest:
   They also serve who only stand and wait.

JOHN MILTON, *SONNETS*

PORTRAIT OF A POET (ARIOSTO?), *Palma Vecchio*

ANNA AND THE BLIND TOBIT, *Gerrit Dou*

THE SHEPHERD'S SONG

✠

HE THAT IS DOWN needs fear no fall,
   He that is low, no pride;
He that is humble ever shall
   Have God to be his guide.

I am content with what I have,
   Little be it or much:
And, Lord, contentment still I crave,
   because Thou savest such.

Fullness to such a burden is
   That go on pilgrimage:
Here little, and hereafter bliss,
   Is best from age to age.

JOHN BUNYAN,
'THE SHEPHERD BOY
SINGS IN THE VALLEY OF HUMILIATION'

SILENCE

AVT TACE
AVT LOQVERE MELIORA
SILENTIO

EITHER BE SILENT, OR SAY SOMETHING BETTER THAN SILENCE

THE INSCRIPTION ON A SELF-PORTRAIT BY SALVATOR ROSA

SELF PORTRAIT, *Salvator Rosa*

SAINT PAUL WRITING, *Pier Francesco Sacchi*

 St Paul on Charity

Though I speak with the tongues of men and of angels, and have not charity, I am become as sounding brass or a tinkling cymbal.

And though I have the gift of prophecy, and understand all mysteries and all knowledge: and though I have all faith, so that I could remove mountains, and have no charity, I am nothing.

And though I bestow all my goods to feed the poor, and though I give my body to be burned, and have not charity, it profiteth me nothing.

Charity suffereth long, and is kind: charity envieth not: charity vaunteth not it self, is not puffed up, doth not behave unseemly, seeketh not her own, is not easily provoked, thinketh no evil, rejoiceth not in iniquity, but rejoiceth in the truth: beareth all things, believeth all things, hopeth all things, endureth all things.

Charity never faileth: but whether there be prophesies, they shall fail; whether there be tongues, they shall cease; whether there be knowledge, it shall vanish away.

For we know in part, and we prophesy in part.

But when that which is perfect is come, then that which is in part, shall be done away.

When I was a child, I spake as a child, I understood as a child, I thought as a child: but when I became a man, I put away childish things.

For now we see through a glass, darkly; but then face to face: now I know in part, but then I shall know even also as I am known. And now abideth faith, hope and charity, these three; but the greatest of these is charity.

I Corinthians XIII,
The King James Version of the Bible

VICES

MY DESTRUCTION
COMETH TO ME OF MYSELF

LANCELOT ANDREWES

THE DEATH OF SAINT PETER MARTYR, *Bernardino da Asola*

Arrogance Condemned

At the same time came the disciples unto Jesus, saying, Who is the greatest in the kingdom of heaven?

And Jesus called a little child unto him, and set him in the midst of them.

And said, Verily I say unto you, Except ye be converted and become as little children, ye shall not enter into the kingdom of heaven.

Whosoever therefore shall humble himself as this little child, the same is greatest in the kingdom of heaven.

And whoso shall receive one such little child in my name receiveth me.

But whoso shall offend one of these little ones which believe in me, it were better for him that a millstone were hanged about his neck, and that he were drowned in the depth of the sea . . .

Take heed that ye despise not one of these little ones: for I say unto you, That in heaven their angels do always behold the face of my Father which is in heaven.

Matthew XVIII,
The King James Version of the Bible

CHRIST BLESSING CHILDREN, *Nicolaes Maes*

SAMSON AND DELILAH, *Peter Paul Rubens*

BETRAYAL

And it came to pass afterward that [Samson] loved a woman in the valley of Sorek, whose name was Delilah.

And the lords of the Philistines came up unto her, and said unto her, Entice him, and see wherein his great strength lieth, and by what means we may prevail against him, that we may bind him to afflict him: and we will give thee every one of us eleven hundred pieces of silver . . .

And it came to pass, when she pressed him daily with her words, and urged him, so that his soul was vexed unto death: that he told her all his heart, and said unto her, There hath not come a rasor upon mine head; for I have been a Nazirite unto God from my mother's womb: if I be shaven, then my strength will go from me, and I shall become weak, and be like any other man.

And when Delilah saw that he had told her all his heart, she sent and called for the lords of the Philistines, saying, Come up this once, for he hath showed me all his heart. Then the lords of the Philistines came up unto her, and brought money in their hand.

And she made him sleep upon her knees; and she called for a man, and she caused him to shave off the seven locks of his head; and she began to afflict him, and his strength went from him.

And she said, The Philistines be upon thee, Samson. And he awoke out of his sleep, and said, I will go out as at other times before, and shake myself. And he wist not that the Lord was departed from him.

But the Philistines took him, and put out his eyes, and brought him down to Gaza, and bound him with fetters of brass; and he did grind in the prison house.

Judges XVI,
The King James Version
of the Bible

THE COVETOUS MAN, *David Teniers the Younger*

COVETOUSNESS

It is a true maxime in Divinity, there is nothing that can suffice the heart of man, but onely Gods grace; where shall you finde the man that saith truly and from his heart he hath enough: When he hath a house he saith, O that I had a little land to it: And when he hath that: He saith, O that I had a Lordship to it, and when he hath that, he saith, O that I had the Mannor that is next to it, or this Office, or that Honour, or one thing or other more; and still as the world growes upon him, his desires grow upon the world, his enough changeth alwaies, every yeare, nay every day, nay every houre he thinks upon another enough; but let a man have grace enough, and he hath all things enough, for Gods grace is alsufficient.

This sufficient grace makes a penny seem to be as big as a shilling, a cottage seem to be as faire as a Pallace, a prison seeme to be as large as a Country, want seeme to be abundance, and nothing to bee all things: This sufficient grace makes us rich in poverty, patient in adversity, strong in weakness, merry in affliction, and hopefull in despaire.

WILLIAM PIERCE

#

DRUNKENNESS is an immoderate affection and use of drink. That I call immoderate that is *besides* or *beyond* that order of good things for which God hath given us the use of drink. The ends are digestion of our meat, cheerfulness and refreshment of our spirits, or any end of health. If at any time we go beside this, or beyond it, it is inordinate and criminal – it is the vice of drunkenness . . .

Drunkenness causeth woes and mischief, wounds and sorrow, sin and shame; it maketh bitterness of spirit, brawling and quarrelling; it increaseth rage and lesseneth strength; it maketh red eyes, and a loose and babbling tongue. It particularly ministers to lust, and yet disables the body; so that in effect it makes man wanton as a satyr, and impotent as age . . .

Its parts and periods are usually thus reckoned: 1. Apish gestures; 2. Much talking; 3. Immoderate laughing; 4. Dulness of sense; 5. Scurrility, that is, wanton, or jeering, or abusive language; 6. An useless understanding; 7. Stupid sleep; 8. Epilepsies, or fallings and reelings, and beastly vomitings . . .

'All things are lawful for me; but I will not be brought under the power of any,' said St Paul. And to be perpetually longing, and impatiently desirous of anything, so that a man cannot abstain from it, is to lose a man's liberty, and to become a servant of meat and drink, or *smoke*.

JEREMY TAYLOR, *RULE AND EXCERCISES OF HOLY LIVING*

DRUNKEN SILENUS SUPPORTED BY SATYRS, *Peter Paul Rubens*

EMULATION AND HATRED

✠

EVERY SOCIETY, corporation, and private family is full of it, it takes hold almost of all sorts of men, from the prince to the ploughman, even amongst gossips it is to be seen, scarce three in a company but there is siding, faction, emulation, between two of them, some *simultas*, jar, private grudge, heart-burning in the midst of them. Scarce two gentlemen dwell together in the country (if they be not near kin or linked in marriage), but there is emulation betwixt them and their servants, some quarrel or grudge betwixt their wives or children, friends and followers, some contention about wealth, gentry, precedency, &c., by means of which, like the frog in Aesop, "that would swell till she was as big as an ox, burst herself at last;" they will stretch beyond their fortunes, callings, and strive so long that they consume their substance in law-suits, or otherwise in hospitality, feasting, fine clothes, to get a few bombast titles, for . . . to outbrave one another, they will tire their bodies, macerate their souls, and through contentions or mutual invitations beggar themselves.

ROBERT BURTON,
ANATOMY OF MELANCHOLY

CORNELIA AND HER SONS, after *Padovanino*

SOLDIERS FIGHTING OVER BOOTY, *Willem Duyster*

GREED

T<small>HE WORKS OF DARKNESS</small> are Repining, Envy, Malice, Covetousness, Fraud, Oppression, Discontent and Violence. All which proceed from the corruption of Men and their mistake in the choice of riches: for having refused those which God made, and taken to themselves treasures of their own, they invented scarce and rare, insufficient, hard to be gotten, little, movable and useless treasures. Yet as violently pursued them as if they were the most necessary and excellent things in the whole world. And though they are all mad, yet having made a combination they seem wise; and it is a hard matter to persuade them either to Truth or Reason. There seemeth to be no way, but theirs; whereas God knoweth they are as far out of the way of Happiness, as the East is from the West.

For, by this means, they have let in broils and dissatisfactions into the world, and are ready to eat and devour one another: particular and feeble interests, false proprieties, insatiable longings, fraud, emulation, murmuring and dissension being everywhere seen; theft and pride and danger, and cousenage, envy and contention drowning the peace and beauty of nature, as waters cover the sea.

T<small>HOMAS</small> T<small>RAHERNE</small>, *C<small>ENTURIES OF</small> M<small>EDITATION</small>*

JEAN DE DINTEVILLE AND GEORGES DE SELVE ('THE AMBASSADORS'), *Hans Holbein the Younger*

PREJUDICE

T HERE IS ANOTHER OFFENCE unto Charity, which no Author hath ever written of, and as few take notice of, and that's the reproach, not of whole professions, mysteries, and conditions, but of whole Nations, wherein by opprobrious Epithets we miscall each other, and by an uncharitable Logick, from a disposition in few, conclude a habit in all.

Le mutin Anglois, et le bravache Escossois;
Le bougre Italien et le fol François;
Le poultron Romain, le larron de Gascongne;
L'Espagnol superbe, et l'Aleman yvrongne.

Saint Paul, that calls the Cretians lyars, doth it but indirectly, and upon quotation of their own Poet. It is as bloody a thought in one as Nero's was in another; for by a word we wound a thousand, and at one blow assassine the honour of a Nation.

THOMAS BROWNE, *RELIGIO MEDICI*

RIGHTEOUSNESS AND SINFULNESS

To thee, o lord, belongeth righteousness, and to me
            confusion of face:
my destruction cometh to me of myself:
        if Thou, Lord, wilt be extreme to mark
                what is done amiss,
        O Lord, who may abide it?
But there is mercy with Thee:
        with God there is mercy,
            with God is plenteous redemption:
and He will deliver from all sins:
        deliver me, O God, from mine,
        deliver my soul from the nethermost hell.
            Deep calleth unto deep
            to deliver from the deep.

LANCELOT ANDREWES, *PRECES PRIVATAE*

THE DREAM (*IL SOGNO*), after *Michelangelo*

TWO TAX GATHERERS, *Marinus van Reymerswaele*

THE RICH MAN

COMES HIS RICHES ILL HIS CREDIT is the Common curse. *Populus sibilat*, the world rails at him living: and when he dies, no man sayes It is pitty, but it is pitty he died not sooner. *They shall not lament* for him, with Ah Lord, or Ah, his Glory. But *hee shall be buried with the burial of an Ass, that hath lived the life of a wolf.* His glorious Tombe erected by his enriched heyre shall bee saluted with execrations and the passengers by will say Here lyes the Devil's Promoter. Comes his wealth well, yet what is credit, of how may we define a good name? Is it to have a Pageant of crindges, and faces acted in a taffeta jacket: To be followed by a world of hang-byes, and howted at by the reeling multitude, like a bird of Paradise, stuck full of py'd feathers: To be daub'd over court-morter, flattery, and set up as a Butt for whores, panders, drunkards, cheaters to shoot their commendations at? To be licked with a sycophants rankling tongue and to have poor men crouch to him, as little dogges use a great mastiff? Is this a good name? Is this credit? Indeed these things may give him a great sound, as the clapper doth a bell, but the bell is hollow. They are empty gulls whose credit is nothing but a great noyse, forced by those lewd clappers.

A rich worldling is like a great Cannon, and flatterers praises are the powder that charge him; whereupon he takes fire and makes a great report, but instantly goes off, goes out in stench.

THOMAS ADAMS

Unwise Marriages

✠

The stags in the greek epigram, whose knees were clog'd with frozen snow upon the mountains, came down to the brooks of the vallies, . . . hoping to thaw their joynts with the waters of the stream; but there the frost overtook them, and bound them fast in ice, till the young heardsmen took them in their stranger snare. It is the unhappy choice of many men, finding many inconveniences upon the mountains of the single life, they descend into the vallies of marriage to refresh their troubles, and there they enter into fetters, and are bound to sorrow by the cords of a mans or womans peevishnesse: and the worst of the evill is, they are to thank their own follies . . .

Let man and wife be carefull to stifle little things, that as fast as they spring, they be cut down and trod upon; for if they be suffered to grow by numbers, they make the spirit peevish and the society troublesome, and the affections loose and easie by an habituall aversation. Some men are more vexed with a flie than with a wound; and when the gnats disturbe our sleep, and the reason is disquieted but not perfectly awakened, it is often seen that he is fuller of trouble than if in the day light of his reason he were to contest with a potent enemy. In the frequent little accidents of a family, a mans reason cannot alwaies be awake; and when his discourses are imperfect, and a trifling trouble makes him yet more restlesse, he is soon betrayed to the violence of passion.

Jeremy Taylor, 'Married Life', *Twenty-five Sermons*

AN ELDERLY COUPLE, *Jan Gossaert* called *Mabuse*

Vice and Old Age

✠

Were there any hopes to outlive vice, or a point to be superannuated from sin, it were worthy of our knees to implore the days of Methuselah. But age doth not rectify, but incurvate our natures, turning bad dispositions into worser habits, and (like diseases,) brings on incurable vices; for every day as we grow weaker in age, we grow stronger in sin, and the number of our days doth but make our sins innumerable. The same vice committed at sixteen, is not the same, though it agree in all other circumstances, at forty, but swells and doubles from the circumstances of our ages, wherein, besides the constant and inexcusable habit of transgressing, the maturity of our judgment cuts off pretence unto excuse or pardon: every sin, the oftner it is committed, the more it acquireth in the quality of evil; as it succeeds in time, so it proceeds in degrees of badness; for as they proceed, they ever multiply, and, like figures in Arithmetick, the last stands for more than all that went before it.

Thomas Browne, *Religio Medici*

PORTRAIT OF AN ELDERLY MAN, *Francesco Bonsignori*

ƉOLUPTUOUSNESS

✠

A LONGING AFTER SENSUAL PLEASURES is a dissolution of the spirit of a man, and makes it loose, soft, and wandering; unfit for noble, wise, or spiritual employments; because the principles upon which pleasure is chosen and pursued are sottish, weak, and unlearned, such as set the body before the soul, the appetite before reason, sense before the spirit, the pleasures of a short abode before the pleasures of eternity.

The nature of sensual pleasure is vain, empty, and unsatisfying, biggest always in expectation, and a mere vanity in the enjoying, and leaves a sting and thorn behind it, when it goes off. Our laughing, if it be loud and high, commonly ends in a deep sigh; and all such pleasures have a sting in the tail, though they carry beauty on the face and sweetness on the lip.

JEREMY TAYLOR, *RULE AND EXCERCISES OF HOLY LIVING*

PARIS AWARDS THE GOLDEN APPLE TO VENUS ('THE JUDGEMENT OF PARIS'), *Peter Paul Rubens*

This World and the Next

So he passed over, and the trumpets sounded for him on the other side

John Bunyan

A PERSONIFICATION OF FAME, *Bernardo Strozzi*

YOUNG MAN HOLDING A SKULL, *Frans Hals*

DEATH BE NOT PROUD

DEATH BE NOT PROUD, though some have called thee
Mighty and dreadfull, for, thou art not soe,
For, those, whom thou think'st, thou dost overthrow,
Die not, poore death, nor yet canst thou kill mee.
From rest and sleepe, which but thy pictures bee,
Much pleasure, then from thee, much more must flow,
And soonest our best men with thee doe goe,
Rest of their bones, and soules deliverie.
Thou art slave to Fate, Chance, kings, and desperate men,
And dost with poyson, warre, and sicknesse dwell,
And poppie, or charmes can make us sleepe as well,
And better than thy stroake: why swell'st thou then?
One short sleepe past, wee wake eternally,
And death shall be no more; death, thou shalt die.

JOHN DONNE

THIS FALLEN WORLD

ON EVERY SIDE we are environed with enemies, surrounded with reproaches, encompassed with wrongs, besieged with offences, receiving evil for good, being disturbed by fools, and invaded with malice. This is the true estate of this world, which lying in wickedness, as our Saviour witnesseth, yieldeth no better fruits, than the bitter clusters of folly and perverseness, the grapes of Sodom, and the seeds of Gomorrah. Blind wretches that wound themselves offend me. I need therefore the oil of pity and the balm of love to remedy and heal them. Did they see the beauty of Holiness or the face of Happiness, they would not do so. To think the world therefore a general Bedlam, or place of madmen, and oneself a physician, is the most necessary point of present wisdom: an important imagination, and the way to Happiness.

THOMAS TRAHERNE, *CENTURIES OF MEDITATION*

THE PHYSICIAN, GIOVANNI AGOSTINO DELLA TORRE, AND HIS SON, NICCOLÒ, *Lorenzo Lotto*

THE RICH MAN BEING LED TO HELL, *David Teniers the Younger*

DIVES AND LAZARUS

✠

THERE WAS A CERTAIN RICH MAN, who was clothed in purple and fine bysse, and fared deliciously every day. And there was a certain beggar, named Lazarus, which lay at his gate full of sores, desiring to be refreshed with the crumbs which fell from the rich man's board. Nevertheless, the dogs came and licked his sores. And it fortuned that the beggar died, and was carried by the angels into Abraham's bosom. The rich man also died, and was buried.

And being in hell in torments, he lift up his eyes and saw Abraham afar off, and Lazarus in his bosom, and he cried and said: father Abraham, have mercy on me, and send Lazarus that he may dip the tip of his finger in water, and cool my tongue: for I am tormented in this flame. But Abraham said unto him, son, remember that thou in thy life time, receivedst thy pleasure, and contrary wise, Lazarus pain. Now therefore he is comforted, and thou art punished. Beyond all this, between you and us there is a great space set, so that they who would go forth from hence to you cannot: neither may come from thence to us.

Then he said: I pray thee therefore, father, send him to my father's house. For I have five brethren: for to warn them, lest they also come into this place of torment. Abraham said unto him: they have Moses and the prophets, let them hear them. And he said, nay father Abraham, but if one came unto them from the dead, they would repent. He said unto him: If they hear not Moses and the prophets, neither will they believe, though one rose from death again.

LUKE XVI, TRANSLATED BY WILLIAM TYNDALE

Mr Valiant-for-Truth Enters Heaven

✠

Said he, I am going to my Fathers, and tho' with great Difficulty I am got hither, yet now I do not repent me of all the Trouble I have been at to arrive where I am. *My Sword*, I give to him that shall succeed me in my Pilgrimage, and my *Courage* and *Skill*, to him that can get it. My *Marks* and *Scars* I carry with me, to be a Witness for me, that I have fought his Battles, who now will be my Rewarder. When the Day that he must go hence, was come, many accompanied him to the River side, into which, as he went, he said, *Death, where is thy Sting?* And as he went down deeper, he said, *Grave, where is thy Victory?* So he passed over, and the Trumpets sounded for him on the other side.

JOHN BUNYAN, *PILGRIMS PROGRESS*

LANDSCAPE: A RIVER AMONG MOUNTAINS, *Netherlandish School*

AN OLD WOMAN WITH A BOOK, *Gabriel Metsu*

GOD BE IN MY HEAD

✠

God be in my head,
And in my understanding;
God be in mine eyes,
And in my looking;
God be in my mouth
And in my speaking;
God be in my heart,
And in my thinking;
God be at my end and at my departing.

ANONYMOUS, SIXTEENTH CENTURY

OF DEATH

✠

Men feare *death*, as Children feare to goe into the darke: And as the Natural Feare in Children, is increased with Tales, so is the other. Certainly, the Contemplation of *Death*, as the *wages of sinne*, and Passage to another world, is Holy, and Religious; But the Feare of it, as a Tribute due unto Nature, is weake. Yet in Religious Meditations, there is sometimes, Mixture of Vanitie, and of Superstition. You shal reade in some of the Friars Books of *Mortification*, that a man should thinke with himselfe, what the Paine is, if he have but his Fingers end Pressed, or Tortured; And thereby imagine, what the Paines of *Death* are, when the whole Body, is corrupted and dissolved; when many times *Death* passeth with lesse paine, than the Torture of a Limme . . .

It is as Naturall to die, as to be borne; And to a little Infant, perhaps, the one, is as painfull, as the other . . .

But above all, beleeve it, the sweetest canticle is, *Nunc dimittis*; when a Man hath obtained worthy Ends, and Expectations. *Death* hath this also; That it openeth the Gate, to good Fame, and extinguisheth Envie.

Francis Bacon, *Essayes*

SAINT DOMINIC, *Giovanni Bellini*

THE SUPPER AT EMMAUS, *Michelangelo Merisi da Caravaggio*

LOVE

Love bade me welcome; yet my soul drew back,
        Guilty of dust and sin,
But quick-ey'd Love, observing me grow slack
        From my first entrance in,
Drew nearer to me, sweetly questioning,
        If I lack'd anything.

'A guest,' I answered, 'worthy to be here':
        Love said, 'You shall be he.'
'I, the unkind, ungrateful? Ah, my dear
        I cannot look on Thee.'
Love took my hand, and smiling did reply,
        'Who made the eyes but I?'

'Truth, Lord, but I have marr'd them; let my shame
        Go where it doth deserve.'
'And know you not,' says Love, 'Who bore the blame?'
        'My dear, then I will serve.'
'You must sit down,' says Love, 'and taste My meat.'
        So I did sit and eat.

GEORGE HERBERT, *The Temple*

PORTRAIT OF AN 83-YEAR-OLD WOMAN, *Rembrandt*

Of the Last Verses in the Book

✠

The seas are quiet, when the winds give o'er;
So calm are we when passions are no more.
For then we know how vain it was to boast
Of fleeting things, so certain to be lost.
Clouds of affection from our younger eyes
Conceal that emptiness which Age descries.

   The soul's dark cottage, batter'd and decay'd,
Lets in new light through chinks that time hath made:
Stronger by weakness, wiser men become
As they draw near to their eternal home:
Leaving the old, both worlds at once they view
That stand upon the threshold of the new.

Edmund Waller

ARDON

At the round earths imagin'd corners, blow
Your trumpets, Angells, and arise, arise
From death, you numberlesse infinities
Of soules, and to your scattred bodies goe,
All whom the flood did, and fire shall o'erthrow,
All whom warre, dearth, age, agues, tyrannies,
Despaire, law, chance, hath slaine, and you whose eyes,
Shall behold God, and never tast deaths woe.
But let them sleepe, Lord, and mee mourne a space,
For, if above all these, my sinnes abound,
'Tis late to aske abundance of thy grace,
When wee are there; here on this lowly ground,
Teach mee how to repent; for that's as good
As if thou hadst seal'd my pardon, with thy blood.

JOHN DONNE

THE BLOOD OF THE REDEEMER, *Giovanni Bellini*

AN OLD MAN HOLDING A PILGRIM-BOTTLE, *Italian School, 17th Century (?)*

Ⓗis Ⓟilgrimage

✠

Give me my scallop-shell of quiet,
   My staff of faith to walk upon;
My scrip of joy, immortal diet,
   My bottle of salvation,
My gown of glory, hope's true gage;
And thus I'll take my pilgrimage.

Blood must be my body's balmer,
   No other balm will there be given;
Whilst my soul, like quiet palmer,
   Travelleth towards the land of heaven;
Over the silver mountains,
Where spring the nectar fountains,
   There will I kiss
   The bowl of bliss;
   And drink mine everlasting fill
   Upon every milken hill.
   My soul will be a-dry before;
   But, after, it will thirst no more.

WALTER RALEGH

℘LEASURE

✠

'TIS MOST UNDOUBTEDLY TRUE, that all Men are equally given to their pleasure; only thus, one man's pleasure lies one way, and another's another . . . He that takes pleasure to hear Sermons, enjoys himself as much as he that hears Plays; and could he that loves Plays endeavour to love Sermons, possibly he might bring himself to it as well as to any other Pleasure. At first it may seem harsh and tedious, but afterwards 'twould be pleasing and delightful. So it falls out in that which is the great Pleasure of some Men, Tobacco; at first they could not abide it, and now they cannot be without it.

Whilst you are upon Earth, enjoy the good Things that are here (to that end were they given) and be not melancholy, and wish yourself in Heaven. If a King should give you the keeping of a Castle, with all things belonging to it, Orchards, Gardens &c., and bid you use them; withal promise you after twenty years to remove you to the Court, and to make you a Privy Councillor; if you should neglect your Castle, and refuse to eat of those fruits, and sit down, and whine, and wish that I was a Privy Councillor, do you think the King would be pleased with you?

JOHN SELDEN, *TABLE TALK*

THE INTERIOR OF THE GROTE KERK, HAARLEM, *Gerrit Berckheyde*

A MUSICAL PARTY, *Jacob Ochtervelt*

A Song
for
St Cecilia's Day

FROM HARMONY, from heavenly harmony
This universal frame began:
When Nature underneath a heap
Of jarring atoms lay,
And could not heave her head,
The tuneful voice was heard from high:—
'Arise, ye more than dead!'
Then cold, and hot, and moist, and dry,
In order to their stations leap,
And music's power obey.
From harmony, from heavenly harmony,
This universal frame began:
From harmony to harmony
Through all the compass of the notes it ran,
The diapason closing full in man.

What passion cannot Music raise and quell?
When Jubal struck the chorded shell,
His listening brethren stood around,
And, wond'ring, on their faces fell
To worship that celestial sound.
Less than a God they thought there could not dwell
Within the hollow of that shell,
That spoke so sweetly and so well.
What passion cannot Music raise and quell?

As from the power of sacred lays,
The spheres began to move,
And sung the great Creator's praise
To all the bless'd above:
So when the last and dreadful hour
This crumbling pageant shall devour,
The trumpet shall be heard on high,
The dead shall live, the living die,
And music shall untune the sky.

JOHN DRYDEN (ABRIDGED)

THE AUTHORS

THOMAS ADAMS (flourished 1612–1653) became preacher at Willington, and after serving as vicar of Wingrave in Buckinghamshire was appointed preacher at St Gregory's under St Paul's Cathedral. In his sermons his evident learning never overwhelms the forcefulness of his Puritan message, so that Robert Southey once compared Adams to Shakespeare himself.

LANCELOT ANDREWES (1555–1626), successively Bishop of Chichester, Ely and Winchester, took part in the translation of the King James Version of the Bible. Learned, wise and marvellously eloquent, when preaching, as John Aubrey put it, 'he did play with his Text, as a Jack-an-apes does, who takes up a thing and tosses and plays with it, and then takes up another, and plays a little with it. Here's a pretty thing, and there's a pretty thing!'

FRANCIS BACON (1561–1626) was a statesman and a lawyer as well as a philosopher. An MP in 1584, Bacon espoused the cause of the Earl of Essex and when Essex fell from grace and rebelled against Elizabeth I turned against him and helped to secure his execution. Knighted in 1603, he became a commissioner for the union of England and Scotland, and in 1607 solicitor-general. His rise, fuelled by his obsequiousness to the monarc hy, was swift. By 1618 he was lord chancellor, by 1621 Viscount St Albans. He lost his positions and influence when convicted of taking bribes. At his death, his debts amounted to £22,000. Alexander Pope justly characterized him as 'the wisest, brightest, meanest of mankind.'

THOMAS BROWNE (1605–1682) studied medicine in France, Italy and England before developing a large and congenial practice based in Norwich. There in 1671 Charles II knighted him. Around 1635 he wrote his *Religio Medici*, a work suffused with learning and spirituality. At first he had no intention of publishing the work. '*Religio Medici* is not to be regarded as a book of philosophic importance,' he wrote. 'It is nothing but a memorial upon me.' But when one of his friends published a pirated edition, Browne decided to let the world see his authentic text.

JOHN BUNYAN (1628–1688) was the son of a Bedfordshire tinker who became an itinerant preacher, often falling foul of the authorities. Imprisoned for twelve years in Bedford gaol, he poured out a torrent of brilliant devotional writings. Released in 1672, he became a licensed preacher, but the toleration initiated by the return of Charles II soon passed and a year later he was tried and again imprisoned, this time for six months. During this imprisonment he began his *Pilgrims Progress*, a masterly allegory of human life recounted as a journey.

ROBERT BURTON (1577–1640), a Leicestershire man, lived his adult life at Christ Church, Oxford. Though Anthony à Wood declared that, 'His company was very merry,' Burton is best known for his *Anatomy of Melancholy*, which first appeared in 1621, where the humour is often decidedly grim.

PATRICK CAREY (flourished 1651), son of the first Lord Falkland, was sent to France at an early age by his mother, who was a Catholic convert. Carey was patronized by Queen Henrietta Maria and Pope Urban VIII, and on his return to England by Sir Edward Hyde (later the Earl of Clarendon). A cavalier and a royalist, his published poems amount to a mere thirty-nine.

ABRAHAM COWLEY (1618–1667) was greatly influenced by the poetry of Edmund Spenser, a volume of which his mother possessed. Cowley wrote his first poems at the age of ten. (They were published when he was fifteen.) Educated at Trinity College, Cambridge, he became a royalist, leaving for Paris in 1646 to serve the exiled queen for twelve years. At the restoration he did not receive his expected preferment, though he lived well enough in the country. He died at Chertsey, according to Alexander Pope of a fever contracted by lying in a field after a bout of drinking.

THOMAS CRANMER (1489–1556) taught divinity at Cambridge and gained the favour of Henry VIII through his advice on the king's desire for a divorce from his first wife Catherine. Cranmer also served as the king's emissary in Italy and Germany. Though cautious, even timid, as Archbishop of Canterbury he promoted the translation of the Bible and himself wrote the first English Prayer Book. Inevitably condemned to death with the return of Catholic monarchy, Cranmer recanted his earlier views no fewer than seven times, but before he was burnt at the stake in Oxford he plunged into the fire the hand that had written his recantations.

JOHN DONNE (c. 1572–1631) was a successful servant of the nobility until he fell from grace by secretly marrying the niece of the Lord Keeper, for which offence he was jailed. The author of scintillating erotic verse, his religious conversion and subsequent ordination led to some of the most passionate sermons and Christian poems of the English-speaking world.

WILLIAM DRUMMOND OF HAWTHORNDEN (1585–1649), a Scotsman who loyally supported Charles I and was mortified by the king's execution, was an inventor as well as a poet, devising machine guns and designing tombs. His legal studies took him as far as Paris and Bourges, and his friendships included Ben Jonson.

JOHN DRYDEN (1631–1700) made his name by writing heroic plays in verse, adapting for this purpose the works of Shakespeare and Milton. Appointed poet laureate and royal historiographer in 1670, he defended the king's cause in a series of savage satires, combining these works with milder, deeply felt religious poetry.

GEORGE HERBERT (1583–1633), of noble birth, after a distinguished public career became parish priest of Bremerton in Wiltshire in 1630 and three years later published a volume of poetry, *The Temple*, which encapsulates piety, mysticism, humility and a deep love of the Church of England and its sacraments. 'I will always condemn my birth, or any title or dignity that can be conferred upon me,' he declared, 'when I shall compare them with my title of being a Priest.'

ROBERT HERRICK (1591–1674), son of a London goldsmith, was apprenticed to his father's trade in 1607 but renounced this six years later to study at St John's College, Cambridge. Ordained to the Anglican ministry, he became vicar of Dean Prior in Devon, but his royalist leanings led to his deprivation in 1647. Herrick regained his living only in 1662. His lyricism gives his verse a unique charm.

JOHN MILTON (1608–1684) began writing superb poetry while still a student at Cambridge. After a visit to Italy, he returned to England and plunged into the polemics of the Civil War, taking the revolutionary side and defending those who had contrived the execution of Charles I. When his defence of divorce was attacked by the Presbyterians he published *Areopagitica*, a passionate defence of a free press. The restoration of the monarchy forced him for some time into hiding. Meanwhile he was developing his project for a poem on *Paradise Lost*, which he began in 1658 and finished in 1663. Milton, who married three times, went blind in 1652.

WILLIAM PIERCE (1580–1670) was a supporter of Archbishop Laud, becoming Bishop of Peterborough in 1630 before being translated to the bishopric of Bath and Wells two years later. Persecuted by the opponents of the monarchy, Pierce was deprived of his living under the Commonwealth but restored in 1660. His fortune (Anthony à Wood records) 'was wheedled away by his second wife – who was too young and cunning for him,' thus impoverishing the children of his first wife.

WALTER RALEGH (1552–1618), navigator, courtier and poet, fought on the Protestant side in

France and Ireland, before becoming a favourite of Queen Elizabeth I. In 1584 he commanded a fleet which colonized part of the American coast, a region which he named Virginia after his patroness. Ralegh returned bringing back potatoes and tobacco. Suspected of intrigue against the queen, in 1592 he was committed to the tower of London, but on his release led a successful expedition to the coast of Trinidad and the Orinoco. Under James I he was again suspected of intrigue against the monarchy and this time was sentenced to death, a sentence commuted to imprisonment in the tower. On his release in 1616 he made another Orinoco expedition. His return and subsequent unpopularity proved disastrous, and in 1656, again out of favour with the monarchy, his earlier death sentence was revived and he was beheaded.

SALVATOR ROSA (1615–1673) was a poet as well as a painter, the author of powerful *Satires*; in consequence of his double talent, this Italian is the only person in this anthology to provide both a text and its accompanying picture.

JOHN SELDEN (1584–1654), antiquary and historian, suffered from the vicissitudes of the seventeenth century, imprisoned twice for his radical views. A member of the Long Parliament, he opposed both the expulsion of bishops from the House of Lords and finally the abolition of episcopacy altogether. Though he continued in office throughout the revolutionary era, he strongly opposed the execution of Charles I.

Recorded by his secretary, Selden's *Table Talk* was published only in 1689, forty-five years after his death.

WILLIAM SHAKESPEARE (1564–1616), born at Stratford-on-Avon, son of a glover and his wife Mary Arden, prospered in London as an actor and dominates the poetry and drama of the Elizabethan and Jacobean ages.

EDMUND SPENSER (1527–1599), after education at Cambridge, joined the circle of wits patronized by Sir Philip Sidney, made a name by publishing his *Shepheards Calendar* in 1578 and consolidated it with the publication of *The Faerie Queene* in 1590. Disappointed in his hopes of preference at the court, he spent disconsolate years in Ireland, consoled however by marriage to Elizabeth Boyle, whom he had wooed with his poem *Amoretti*, celebrating their nuptials in his eloquent *Epithalamion*. Spenser's Irish castle was burned down during an insurrection, his youngest child dying in the conflagration.

JEREMY TAYLOR (1613–1667), chaplain to Archbishop Laud, three times imprisoned during the Civil War which saw the execution of his master, became Bishop of Down and Connor after the restoration of the monarchy. His ornately matchless prose, worldly-wise yet impassionedly devout, graces above all his *Rule and Excercises of Holy Living*, which was published in 1640, and his *Rule and Excercises of Holy Dying*, published in 1651.

THOMAS TRAHERNE (c.1636–1674), the son of a Hereford shoemaker, studied at Brasenose College, Oxford, and in 1667 was appointed chaplain to Sir Orlando Bridgeman, lord keeper of the great seal, retaining the living of Credenhill, just outside Hereford. His *Centuries of Meditation* was written for his friend Mrs Susannah Hopton who had set up a little society in Herefordshire to study and practise heartfelt religion.

WILLIAM TYNDALE (died 1536), educated both at Oxford and at Cambridge, announced his intention of translating the Bible into English with the claim that, 'If God spared his life ere many years he would cause a boy that driveth the plough to know more of the scripture than he did.' In 1524 he was in Wittenberg, where he met Martin Luther. The following year, in Cologne, he was supervising the first edition of his translation of the New Testament. Denounced by his enemies, with many copies of his translation publicly burned, Tyndale fled to Marburg and the protection of its Protestant prince. Eventually moving to Antwerp, he met his death when a young Englishman named Henry Phillips professed sympathy for the Reformation, decoyed Tyndale from his house and handed him over to the Imperial authorities. Condemned as a heretic, Tyndale was strangled and then burned at the stake. His last words were, 'Lord, open the king of England's eyes.'

EDMUND WALLER (1606–1687), educated at Eton and Cambridge, became a member of parliament during the Civil War and in 1643 was expelled from the House of Commons for an alleged conspiracy. Fined £10,000 and banished, he was allowed to return home only in 1651.

HENRY WOTTON (1568–1639) was a diplomat as well as a poet, serving James I as ambassador to Venice for almost twenty years and coining the epigram that an ambassador is an honest man sent abroad to lie for the good of his country. He died, wrote Izaak Walton, 'worthy of the love and favour of so many Princes, and Persons of eminent Wisdom and Learning, worthy of the trust committed unto him, for the Service of his Prince and Country.'

Acknowledgements

✠

The publishers would like to thank the National Gallery, London for supplying transparencies for all the paintings in the book.

Editor's Regrets

ALAS, SPACE WAS NOT FOUND for all the writings I should like to have included. I am happy to squeeze in here a quotation from John Aubrey, the seventeenth-century antiquarian and snapper-up of unconsidered trifles, illustrating the virtue of friendship. Aubrey records of Bishop Richard Corbet of Oxford and his chaplain Dr Lushington:

One time, as he was confirming . . . being to lay his hand on the head of a man very bald, he turns to his Chaplaine, Lushington, and sayd, *Some Dust, Lushington* (to keep his hand from slipping). There was a man with a great venerable Beard: sayd the Bishop, *You, behind the Beard*.

His Chaplaine, Dr Lushington, was a very learned and ingeniose man, and they loved one another. The Bishop sometimes would take the key of the wine-cellar, and he and his Chaplaine would goe and lock themselves in and be merry. Then first he layes downe his Episcopall hat – *There lyes the Doctor*. Then he putts off his gowne – *There lyes the Bishop*. Then 'twas, *Here's to thee, Corbet*, and *Here's to thee, Lushington*.

The last words he sayd were, *Good night, Lushington.*'